OLD SHANGHAI
A PHOTOGRAPHIC ALBUM

老　上　海　风　景

上海人民美術出版社
SHANGHAI PEOPLE'S FINE ARTS PUBLISHING HOUSE

前　　　言

汤 伟 康

老上海，这座城市的传奇过于复杂：十里洋场、冒险家的乐园、远东第一大埠、风云际会的政治大舞台……众说纷纭，莫衷一是。从20世纪初，随着上海在中国沿海城市现代化进程中扮演着愈来愈重要角色的同时，她也被包括历史学者在内的世人瞩目、研究和解读。百年后的今天，怀旧和追溯老上海风物成为时尚。这些看似支离破碎、关联不大的老照片，分门别类，加注释文，编成一本老上海影集，恰恰可以满足读者熟悉上海滩昔日风貌、探究这座城市现代化进程的需求，从而领略和认知今日上海日新月异的变迁。

西方学者总喜欢把上海说成是"从一个小渔村突然发展成一个大都市"。其实，上海宋代设镇，早在南宋咸淳三年（公元1207年）之前，位于黄浦江西岸的上海镇就曾设市舶司（船运、贸易税收机构），管理对外贸易。上海元代设县，除盐业和海运继续发展，同时也是棉花种植和棉纺织手工业的先进地区，为明代江南地区棉纺织业的繁荣作出了贡献。明代中晚期，我国商品经济发展，促进了资本主义萌芽的产生。上海地区交通发达、经济繁荣、文化活跃，日益发展成为国内外贸易的重要地区。乾隆年间，上海恢复了航海运输，又取得了"南吴壮县""江海通津"的地位。上海县城内河上有桥，浜里有船；水是活水，城是青城，一派田园城市风光。

鸦片战争的炮火与中英《南京条约》的签订，把一个主权独立的中国逐步变为半封建半殖民地的国家。1843年11月，上海被迫对外开埠，

英、法、美等国先后在上海开辟租界，并不断向界外蚕食扩张，至20世纪20年代，已初步形成了英美联合的公共租界和法租界并存的城市格局，俨然成为一个"国中之国"。

开埠以后，上海原有的自我封闭的经济格局被打破，外国商人蜂拥而至，各国洋行纷纷设立，上海市场开始与国际市场联系起来。近代上海的金融典当、钱庄、银号、票号、银行，以及信托公司、金融性交易所、保险公司等，运用各种经营方式以适应不同的业务

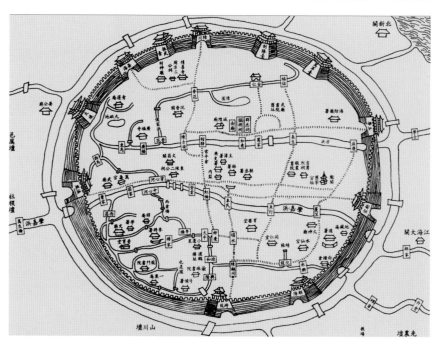

清同治年间上海县城图　Map of Shanghai at Years of Tongzhi, Qing Dynasty

需要，从而推动着上海发展成国际金融中心。显著的表征是外滩成了"中国的华尔街"。中外金融帝国坐落于此，连带许多城市功能汇集于此，怡和洋行等公司众多码头设立于此，黄浦江上各国货轮云集。在外滩，看得见万国国旗。外国商人在这里有自己的俱乐部，其中最早和最具标志性的是1864年英国商人在外滩成立的上海总会。毗邻且与外滩平行的江西路，串起了香港路、宁波路、北京路、天津路、南京路、九江路、汉口路、福州路、广东路，也在近百年里迅猛发展。这里不但聚集多家外资银行，还集中了近百家国内银行总部。外滩一带变成了当时欧洲以外最欧洲化的街区。这里的建筑缺乏整体规划，是暴发户们一掷千金的产物，由此被欧洲老贵族讥讽为"万国建筑博览会"。

《老上海风景》跨页展示若干帧外滩长卷，真实写照外滩从19世纪80年代至20世纪三四十年代的整体变迁，避免读者被外滩林林总总的其他历史图影带入只见树木不见森林的误区。外滩的重要，必然使之充满了政治性。租界的重要仪式都在这里举行，各式各样的人都曾经希望用自己的历史观来讲述关于外滩的故事，以至外滩的纪念碑、塑像不断地被矗立、推倒。外滩又是富有象征意义的地方，各国领事馆大多设立在这里，向人们显示对这座城市的影响。20世纪中西混杂的近代上海历史源于外滩。

与外滩相望的是上海的母亲河"苏州河"，上海滩是从哪里生长出来的，有人说是黄浦江，其实不然，苏州河（吴淞江）才是孕育上海的母亲河。苏州河除了河口发育和生长年代先于黄浦江，重要因素还在于她是联通富庶江南地区和上海贸易的孔道。许多上海市民原是从江南鱼米之乡经苏州河进入上海，转为近代城市市民。苏州河上还有以外白渡桥为代表的座座桥梁，展现各异风景，又同城市发展构成复杂的关系。岸边拥有众多市政设施和工厂、码头的苏州河，是上海城市的主动脉。

上海开埠通商，租界兴起，人口剧增，不但刺激了城市商业的极大繁荣，而且加剧了她的资本主义化进程。20世纪20年代始，上海已成为万商云集的国际都会。从此时起，以南京路为代表的商业街取代了广东路、福州路，成为名副其实的"大马路"。当时上海售卖环球百货的"四大公司"全部都坐落在南京路上，南京路执上海乃至全中国商业之牛耳，被中外旅游者认为是中国商业精神的代表，现代生活方式的窗口。

上海开埠以后，市政建设突飞猛进，交通工具的更迭日新月异，交通运输和西式通讯设备推陈出新。早在1850年代，上海马路上就开始行驶的西式亨斯美马车，取代了传统的人力轿子。1870年代，上海又从日本引进人力车（黄包车）。20世纪初，上海英租界开始出现有轨电车，法租界和华界跟进与仿效。此后，无轨电车、公共汽车先后面世，私家轿车、出租车，脚踏人力车（三轮车）和自行车如雨后春笋般涌入街头，新旧交通工具你方唱罢我登场，成为独特的城市景观，以西方市政管理模式为标准的新型交通规则应运而生，拉近了人与人之间的距离，也加快了社会的开化和风尚的转移。

随着上海都市化进程的加快，作为太平洋西岸的环球贸易中心，上海愈来愈赢得欧美人的青睐。外侨移居上海的持续不断，给上海增添了异彩。随之，上海居民外出方式呈现快速更新、都市性日趋鲜明的特色。在"欧风美雨"的飘打下，上海的社会风俗发生了令人瞩目的变化，上海本地风俗以及各地移民带来的风俗在上海都市的时空中日益嬗蜕，并形成新的都市习俗。

近代上海不仅是中国最大的工商都市，而且是中国最重要的政治舞台。一代又一代的仁人志士，用自己的鲜血和生命换来了上海的今天。1949年5月12～27日，在上海市民的有力配合下，上海终于解放，汉口路上的上海市政府大楼顶上升起了第一面五星红旗。

历史图影能传真丰沛的历史生活情景。《老上海风景》贮存着上海这座城市里的一幢幢建筑、一条条马路、一个个人物、一组组群体、一种种表情……人文气息浓厚、生活细节真切，这样的图册，完全能让读者在阅读中解开老上海城市谜团，领略这座如万花筒般的城市风物、风情和风貌。

甲午年早春，记于上海香榭丽花园寓所

Foreword

Tang Weikang

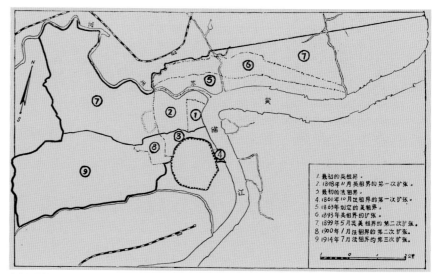

上海租界扩张示意图　Maps on the expansion of concessions in Shanghai

The old Shanghai was a legendary city with its unique sophistication. In people's memory, Shanghai was the wonderland of adventurers, the largest seaport over the Far East and the miracle stage of politicians. Since the beginning of the 20th century, Shanghai has been playing a increasingly important role in the modernization of Chinese coastal cities, and has been constantly studied and interpreted by scholars all over the world. Nowadays, people's reminiscence over old Shanghai has already become a trend. Many photos recording the past of Shanghai, though seem fragmented at a first glance, once compiled, organized and footnoted, can be well served in introducing the history and scenery of old Shanghai. Through the book *Old Shanghai: A Photographic Ablum*, people can have a better understanding of the modernization of Shanghai thus be able to appreciate the incessant change of the metropolis.

Scholars of the West always regard Shanghai as "a metropolis developed from a fishing village". In fact, the origin of Shanghai was much more than a fishing village. Shanghai Town was established in Song Dynasty. As early as 1207 A.D, a shipping tax bureau was set up in order to administrate foreign trade. In Yuan Dynasty, Shanghai County was established and its salt industry and shipping continue to develop. During

this period, cotton production and textile industry in Shanghai had contributed a lot in booming the textile production of regions south of Yangtze River. In the middle and late period of Ming Dynasty, China's commodity economy began to prosper and capitalism started to sprout. Thanks to its convenient transportation, vibrant economy and dynamic culture, Shanghai became a key area of domestic and foreign trade. During Qianlong period(1736-1795), Shanghai resumed its shipping transportation and gained the reputation of "Wealthy Watertown in South Wu area". The city of Shanghai was all connected by the creeks, bridges and boats.

The outbreak of Opium War and the signing of *Treaty of Nanking* turned China into half-colonial half-feudal. In November 1843, Shanghai was forced to opened its seaport to foreign powers. Britain, France and America successively established and expanded their foreign settlements in Shanghai. In 1920s, Shanghai was turned into a "state within a state" where British-American Public Settlement and French Settlement stood side by side in the city.

After opening its seaport to outside world, the original closed economic pattern of Shanghai was broken. Foreign businessmen rushed into the city; foreign firms began to emerge; Shanghai's market was opened to the

International market. Banks, financing corporations and insurance companies continued to drove Shanghai into a global financial center. A notable representation of all these trends was the Bund, known as the "China Wall Street", where financing giants, foreign companies, docks and cargo ships gathered. Different national flags fluttered on top of the buildings. Clubs owned by foreign businessmen were also constructed here. Among these clubs, the earliest and largest one is the Shanghai Club constructed by British businessmen in 1864. Jiangxi Road, paralleled to the Bund and connected Hong Kong Road, Ningbo Road, Nanjing Road and several other key roads of Shanghai, was also highly developed in the past century. Both foreign banks and domestic banks gathered in this area. Overnight millionaires from the West spent huge sum of money to construct European style buildings, thus making the Bund the most Europeanized block outside Europe. Thus the Bund was ridiculed by traditional European aristocrats as the "exhibition of the world's architecture" for its lack of serious planning.

Old Shanghai: A Photographic Album contains many panoramic photos of the Bund from 1980s to 1940s, which help readers to understand the overall transformation of the Bund, rather than only catching a few fragments in the whole history. The importance of the Bund owes a lot to its political nature: important ceremonies in the settlements were all held in here. All kinds of important figures at that time wanted to tell the story of the Bund with their own historical perspective. Thus many monuments were constructed and torn down over and over again. The Bund is also a symbolic place where consulates of different countries were established to demonstrate their influences in Shanghai. In a word, the hybrid modern history of Shanghai was rooted in the Bund.

Suzhou Creek, connected with the Bund and Huangpu River, is the "mother river" of Shanghai. Some people regard Huangpu River as the origin of Shanghai. Actually Suzhou Creek is the one that breed Shanghai. Besides the earlier estuary development, more important factor is that as the channel connecting Shanghai with other rich South region of China, Suzhou Creek created opportunities for trade and helped numerous people from those wealthy regions flowed into Shanghai. The famous Garden Bridge and other different styles of bridges connect the whole city and contribute to its fast development. Factories, facilities and docks are located near Suzhou Creek, making it the artery of Shanghai.

The opening of the seaport and the establishment of foreign settlements in Shanghai boosted its population and stimulated its economy. Shanghai had become a metropolis with innumerable business firms. Nanjing Road, which later became the largest commercial street in Shanghai, took its shape under that situation. The "Big Four Department Stores" were all located here. Nanjing Road was leading in business throughout China and was regarded as the representative of Chinese entrepreneurial spirit and modern lifestyle.

Shanghai's urban construction had been advanced rapidly since the opening of the seaport. Means of transportation and communication progressed dramatically. As early as 1850s, western carriages had replaced sedan chairs on the street of Shanghai; in 1870s, Japanese rickshaw was introduced; in 1900s, streetcars began to appear in British Settlements, French Settlements and Chinese Residential Area. After that, wireless streetcars, buses, private cars, taxis, tricycles and bicycles all sprung up like bamboo shoots. New traffic rules under Western administration system brought people closer together and accelerated the transformation of social customs.

As the trading center in Asia-Pacific regions, Shanghai gained huge popularity among Westerners, thanks to its fast urbanization. An increasing amount of foreigners came to Shanghai and injected new energy into the city. Shanghai became more dynamic and diversified. Under the European and American fashion trend, the local custom and different cultures of the foreigners mixed together and became a brand new urban culture.

Modern Shanghai was not only the largest industrial and commercial city in China, but also the most important political stage. Generations of people with lofty ideals sacrificed their own blood and lives for the today's new Shanghai. From May 15th to 27th, 1947, under the strong cooperation of Shanghai citizens, Shanghai finally achieved liberation and the first Five-Star Red Flag was finally raised on top of the building of the municipal government of Shanghai.

Historical images can deliver of Shanghai's history and life style. *Old Shanghai: A Photographic Album* has collected numerous buildings, road, individuals, groups and facial expressions that can help people decoding the mystery of Old Shanghai. Filled with rich cultural flavor and vivd details, this book, like a kaleidoscope, will present you the sceneries, features and customs of a brilliant Old Shanghai.

[Written in Champs-Elysees Apartment, spring of 2014]

老城厢
OLD CITY TOWN

老上海风景　OLD SHANGHAI: A PHOTOGRAPHIC ALBUM

1850年代的上海县城墙。上海建县于元至元二十八年（1291年），明嘉靖三十二年（1553年）为抵御倭寇侵扰，修筑城墙。城周长九里，高二丈四尺，城墙外有六丈宽的护城河，设六处城门和三处水门。

The city wall of Shanghai county in the 1850s. Shanghai county was established in 1291. In 1553, the city wall, built to defend the Japanese pirates, had a circumference of 4.5 kilometers, a height of 7.2 meters with a moat 18 meters wide. There were altogether six city gates and three water gates.

清末上海县城门下的集市。
The market under the city gate of Shanghai County in the 1850s.

1860年代位于上海县城内的豫园湖心亭和九曲桥。

The mid-lake pavilion and the zig-zag bridge of Yuyuan Garden in the county of Shanghai in the 1860s.

1860年代上海县城的老北门外。

The old north gate of Shanghai County in the 1860s.

1920年代上海县城内的居民用消防栓给水。

Shanghai citizens taking water from the fire cock in the 1920s.

1860年代上海县城新北门街景。

The street view of the new North Gate of Shanghai county in the1860s.

Native City Street S'hai

1930年代上海县城内街景。

The view of the street inside Shanghai county in the 1930s.

1910年代上海县城内街景。
The view of the street inside Shanghai county in the 1910s.

THE BUND & SUZHOU CREEK

老上海风景　OLD SHANGHAI: A PHOTOGRAPHIC ALBUM

1892年的外滩。洋行和住宅鳞次栉比，黄浦江上商船往返频繁，江畔码头林立，一片繁忙景象。

Foreign firms and residences were orderly arranged in Puxi while merchant boats and docks were dispersed on Huangpu River. Photo taken in 1892.

1870年代，雪后的公共租界外滩。左边为1861年的英国人创办的上海总会，带阳台的3层楼房，砖木结构，红砖墙，东印度式建筑。1879年5月，美国总统格兰特卸任后访问中国，英侨在此开舞会招待他。

The Bund after snow in the 1870s. The building on the left was the Shanghai Club set up by the British in 1861. It is a post and panel structure building designed in East Indian style. In May 1879, when the retired American president Grant came to China, the British held a party to welcome him.

1880年代公共租界外滩街景。随着租界的设立，从吴淞江到县城的纤道已成为宽阔的马 路，行驶着马车和人力车，道路两旁为林立的洋行和商业码头。图中最高的建筑为建于1874 年的汇丰银行新楼。

The view of the Bund in the 1880s. The once narrow path from Suzhou Creek to the county of Shanghai had become wide roads with carriages and rickshaws coming through. Foreign firms and docks were on either side of the road. The highest building on the left was the building of Hong Kong and Shanghai Banking Corporation.

1869年，吴淞江下游和黄浦江汇合处，南面的涨滩刚刚形成。

The Bund on the joint of Suzhou Creek and Huangpu River in the British Settlement in 1869.

1900年代繁忙的法租界外滩十六铺码头。
The bustling Shiliupu Dock on the French Bund in the 1900s.

1930年代的法租界外滩十六铺码头。
The Shiliupu Dock of the French Bund in the 1930s.

1910年代的公共租界外滩，从杨树浦到外滩的3路有轨电车。

The wheelbarrow, rickshaw and streetcar on the Bund in the 1910s.

Shanghai. The Bund in Front of the Shanghai Club.

1910年代的公共租界外滩街景，左边为上海总会。

The view of the street of the Bund in the 1910s, on the left was Shanghai Club.

位于南京东路公共租界外滩的巴夏礼铜像。巴夏礼（Parkes Sir Harry Smith, 1828-1885），英国外交官，1862年任上海领事。铜像立于1890年4月8日，上海沦陷后被日军拆除。

The sculpture of Sir Harry Smith Parkes on the Bund. Sir Harry Smith Parkes (1828-1855) was a British diplomatist. In 1862 he became the consul of Shanghai. The sculpture was built on April 8th, 1890, and was torn apart by the Japanese troops after the fall of Shanghai.

1920年代，停泊在黄浦江上的趸船，是西方列强在上海进行鸦片贸易的储藏、分装、交易场所。
A wharf boat on Huangpu River in the 1920s. Western powers used wharfs to store and trade opium.

1930年代，位于公共租界外滩海关大楼前的赫德铜像。赫德（Hart Sir Robert，1835- 1911），1863年11月起任中国海关总税务司，掌管中国海关达40年。铜像立于1913年，上海沦陷后被日军拆除。

The sculpture of Sir Robert Hart on the Bund. Sir Robert Hart was a British who became the Customs Commissioner and took charge of the customs of China for 40 years. The sculpture was built in 1913 and was torn apart by the Japanese troops after the fall of Shanghai. Photo was taken in the 1930s.

1900年代的外滩。右边有尖塔的城堡式建筑为德国总会，1908年建成，高3层，巴洛克式砖木结构，楼顶有两个不同形式的巴洛克式塔楼，1934年拆除。1937年在原址上建立中国银行。

The the Bund in the 1900s. On the left was German Club with a spire. Completed in 1908, the building was constructed in post and panel structure and had altogether three floors. In 1934, it was torn down and replaced by the Bank of China later in 1937.

1857年，清政府在公共租界外滩设江海北关，为衙门式木结构建筑，1891年为翻建新江海北关，大楼被拆除。
The old Customs House on the Bund in 1857. It was designed in traditional Chinese Yamen style.

1893年，在中国原衙门式建筑原址上改建竣工的江海北关，英国教堂风格，砖木结构，中间有5层高的哥特式方形钟楼。
The old Customs House was later torn town by Qing Government and was replaced by a church style building in1893.

1890年代福州路公共租界外滩的汇丰银行大楼，右边为1893年新建的海关钟楼。汇丰银行开办于1865年4月，是第一家总行设在中国的外国银行。

The building of Hong Kong-Shanghai Banking Corporation on the Bund in the 1890s. On the right was the new bell tower of the Customs House built in 1893. Hong Kong-Shanghai Banking Corporation was founded in April 1865 and was the first foreign bank which base was set in China.

汇丰银行新大楼，建成于1923年，英国人称为"从苏伊士运河到远东东白令海峡最华贵的建筑"。右边的新海关大楼建于1927年，外观为希腊式新古典主义风格。摄于1930年代。

The new base of HSBC built in 1923. It was praised by the British as "the most beautiful and elegant building from the Suez Canal to the Bering Strait in the Far East". And the new Customs House was built in 1927. Photo taken in the 1930s.

1900年公共租界外滩景色。图中钟楼建筑为江海北关，海关左边是汇丰银行，远处尖顶为圣三一教堂。

The Bund in 1900. The bell tower was the Customs House , the one on the left it was Hong Kong-Shanghai Banking Corporation, far away was the Holy Trinity Church.

1910年代的公共租界北外滩虹口码头。
The Hongkou Dock of the Bund in the 1910s.

[042] 位于公共租界外滩延安东路口的欧战和平纪念碑。第一次世界大战，上海部分外国侨民回国参战，此碑为纪念战死者所立，碑上刻有"功炳欧西，名留华夏"铭文和死者姓名。上海沦陷后被日军拆毁。图为1924年2月纪念碑落成仪式。

[042] The WWI Peace Monument located in the Bund. In the first World War, some of the foreigners came back to their countries to attend the battle, and the monument was for the death of war. On the monument inscribed "gong bing ou xi, ming liu hua xia" (winning the battle in Europe and the reputation in China) and the names of the deceased. The monument was torn down by the Japanese. The photo was taken during the inauguration of the monument in Feburary 1924.

[043] 公共租界外滩信号台和法租界十六铺码头，黄浦江上停泊着外国军舰，左下角为欧战纪念碑。外滩延安东路口信号台，建成于1907年3月9日。塔顶旗杆上悬挂不同标记，告知黄浦江上往来船只天气情况。

[043] The signal tower on the junction of East Yan'an Road and the Bund. Built in March 9th, 1907. The tower was used to tell the weather to the ships on the river by hanging up different signals on the tower.

1910年代的公共租界外滩，中间为1906年重建的汇中饭店，后面的尖顶塔楼是德国总会。

The Bund in the 1910s.,in the middle was renovated Palace Hotel in 1906. The tower behind it was the German Club.

1930年代公共租界的外滩。当时最高建筑为建于1927年的沙逊大厦。
The Bund in the 1930s. The tallest building was Sassoon Mansions built in 1927.

1925年的外滩全景，照片中除新的海关大楼、沙逊大厦和中国银行、百老汇大厦外，外滩主要建筑都已建成，整体轮廓已经成形。

A full view of the Bund in 1925. All the buildings except the new Customs House, Sassoon Mansion,Bank of China and Broadway Mansions were completed.

公共租界外滩中国通商银行门口进行消防演习，摄于清末。
Fire fighting drill in front of the Commercial Bank of China, in the 1910s.

1929年的公共租界外滩。
The Bund in1929.

[052] 1930年代的公共租界外滩，码头密集，车水马龙，一片繁荣， 1927-1937年是上海发展的黄金10年。图中右边为欧战纪念碑。

[052] The Bund in the1930s. The docks were gathered and the road was filled with vehicles. 1927 to 1937 was the prime time of the development of Shanghai. The monument on the right side of the photo was the WWI Monument.

[053] 1940年代的外滩，此时的公共租界外滩的主要建筑全部建成，远处华懋饭店（沙逊大厦）后面的中国银行于1937年落成。此时欧战纪念碑已被日军拆除。

[053] The Bund in the 1940s. Most of the buildings were already completed, within which the Bank of China was completed in 1937.

A panoramic view of the Famous
Waterfront of Shanghai No. 2

A panoramic view of the Famous Waterfront of Shanghai, No. 1

1930年代的外滩、黄浦江全景。照片中除中国银行外，新的海关大楼、华懋饭店（沙逊大厦）、百老汇大厦都已建成，外滩建设接近尾声。此时，浦东的码头、货栈日渐增多。

The full view of the Bund in the 1930s. The Customs House, Sassoon Mansion and the Broadway Mansion were already been built. The Architectural Complex on the Bund was nearly completed(except for the Bank of China), and there were more and more docks and warehouses on the other side of Huangpu River.

1930年代苏州河下游鸟瞰，由近及远依次为乍浦路桥、四川路桥、江西路桥、河南路桥。

A bird's eye view of the downstream of Suzhou Creek in 1930s. The bridges from near to far were Zhapu Road Bridge, Sichuan Road Bridge and Henan Road Bridge.

1930年代的外白渡桥，中间为洋人的划艇俱乐部。
Garden Bridge in the 1930s. In the middle was the Canoe Club.

A panoramic view of the Famous
Waterfront of Shanghai, No. 4

A Panoramic view of the Famous Waterfront of Shanghai, No. 3

[060] 位于苏州河乍浦路桥南堍的光陆大戏院，建成于1926年。

[060] Capital Theatre located on the junction of Suzhou Creek and Zhapu Road, completed in 1926.

[061] 苏州河北岸的河滨大楼，建成于1935年，是上海建筑面积最大的一座美国公寓式大楼，为现代实用主义风格。

[061] Riverside Mansion on the north side of Suzhou Creek was built in 1933, it was the largest American style apartment in Shanghai. The apartment was built upon modern pragmatism style.

1950年代的苏州河。
Suzhou Creek, in the1950s.

1948年，上海解放前夕，苏州河上挤满了逃难的船只，远处是外白渡桥。
Suzhou Creek was crowded with boats the day before the liberation of Shanghai. Faraway was the Garden Bridge.

百老汇大厦、位于外白渡桥北堍，1930年动工建造，1934年建成，为早期现代派风格建筑。

The Broadway Mansion on the north of Garden Bridge. Completed in 1934, the style of the building was constructed in early modernism.

1950年代的黄浦江、苏州河口。

The junction of Huangpu River and Suzhou Creek, in the 1950s.

Shanghai — Yang King Pang.

19世纪末洋泾浜上的木船。洋泾浜为黄浦江支流，英法租界界河，北面为英租界、南面为法租界。1941年11月，填浜筑路，定名为爱亚多路，今名延安东路。

Wooden boat on Yangjingbang creek. Yangjingbang, the tributary of Huangpu River, was the border of the British and French Settlement. In the November of 1941, the creek was filled up and became a road, which is the current Yan'an Road

1930年代的爱亚多路，远处为外滩。
The Edward Avenue (current Yan'an Road) in the 1930s. Far away was the Bund

老上海风景　OLD SHANGHAI: A PHOTOGRAPHIC ALBUM

公共租界侨民庆祝英王诞辰。

The British celebrating the birthday of the King in the public concessions.

1901年7月16日，清廷醇亲王载沣一行，经上海前往德国为德驻华公使被杀事件道歉。图为经过南京路时情景。
On July 16th ,the prince of Qing Dynasty and his entourage went all the way from Shanghai to Germany to apologize for the killing of the diplomat of Germany. Photo taken in Nanjing Road.

1900年代的南京路。

Nanjing Road in the 1900s.

Shanghai. Nanking Roa

1930年代南京路上的邵万生南货店和老凤祥银楼。
The Shao Wansheng Department Store and the Laofengxiang Silver Store on Nanjing Road, in the 1930s.

1900年代南京路上的亨达利钟表店。

The Hope Brother's & Co. on Nanjing Road, in the 1910s.

1920年代南京路上的先施公司（右）和永安公司。

The Sincere Corporation and the Wing-On Corporation on Nanjing Road in the 1920s.

1930年代的南京路街景，中间的尖塔从至左至右分别为永安公司、新新公司和先施公司。

The view of Nanjing Road in the 1930s, the towers from left to right were Wing-On Corporation, Sun Sun Corporation and Sincere Corporation.

南京路上的七重天永安新厦。永安新厦建成于1933年，美国现代摩天大楼建筑风格。
The Seventh Heaven Tower (new Wing-On Tower) on Nanjing Road, in the 1930s.

1930年代南京路街景。
The view of Nanjing Road in the 1930s.

大光明电影院，享有"远东第一影院"的盛名，它始建于1928年，1932年，由著名的匈牙利建筑师邬达克设计重建。
Grand Theatre in the 1930s. Having the reputation of the No.1 theatre in the Far East, Grand Theatre was built in 1928. In 1932 it was redesigned by the famous Hungarian architect Hudek.

1930年代行驶在南京路上的有轨电车。

The streetcar on Nanjing Road in the 1930s.

1930年代外滩南京路口。
The junction of the Bund and the Nanjing Road in the 1930s.

1930年代位于南京路、西藏路口的荣昌祥西服店和新新公司。
The RongChangxiang Store and Sun Sun Corporation on Nanjing Road in the 1930s.

1936年在原荣昌祥西服店址上建成大新公司，（现上海市第一百货商店）。

The Sun Corporation was built on the original address of the RongChangxiang Store in 1936. It is the current No.1 Department Store of Shanghai.

1930年代，跑马厅观看赛马的观众和骑手。

The jockey and the spectators in the Race Club in the 1930s.

1930年代的跑马厅鸟瞰。左边的国际饭店1933年10月竣工，为当时上海及远东的最高建筑。跑厅周边是如蜂巢般的石库门弄堂民居。

A bird's eye view of the Race Club, the building on the left was Park Hotel, the tallest at that time in Shanghai, the tall buildings were surrounded by Shikumen buildings.Photo was taken in 1930s.

1930年代南京路由东向西鸟瞰，此时大新、新新、永安和先施四大公司均已建成，南京路为上海乃至全国最繁华的商业街，远处为国际饭店。

A bird's eye view of Nanjing Road from east to west in the 1930s, at that time, the big four companies in Shanghai, Sincere, Wing-On, Sun Sun and the Sun had all completed, making Nanjing Road the most flourishing commercial street in China. Faraway was the Park Hotel.

1930年代南京路由西向东鸟瞰，中间为建成于1936年的大新公司。

A bird's eye view of Nanjing Road from west to east, in the middle was the base of Sun Corporation built in 1936. Photo was taken in the 1930s.

国际饭店，1934年建成，24层，82米高，现代摩天大楼建筑风格，为当时远东最高建筑。

Park Hotel completed in 1934, Park Hotel is a modern skyscraper with 24 floors (82 meters). It was at that time the tallest building in the far east.

1932年的华懋饭店（沙逊大厦），位于南京路外滩，1926年开工建造，1929年建成，13层，77米高，现代摩天大楼建筑风格。

Sassoon Mansion was a modern skyscraper built in 1929 with a height of 77 meters (13 floors). Photo was taken in 1932.

华懋公寓，位于今长乐路、茂名南路口，1925年动工建造，1929年建成，为现代风格的高层公寓。

Cathay Mansion located on the junction of Changle Road and South Maoming Road. Completed in 1929, it was built as a modern apartment.

大世界歌楽場 る遊調情那支な的索大 (海 上)
Daisekai Arcadia, Shanghai.

1930年代的大世界游乐场，位于西藏中路，为上海最大的综合游乐场，电影、马戏、赌场、剧场等各种游乐项目应有尽有。因游客众多，商家广告投放也非常密集。

The Great World Entertainment Center, located on Middle Xizang Road, was the biggest entertaining club in Shanghai with all kinds of items such as cinema, circus, gambling and theatre. There were a huge amount of advertisements in the club because of the huge flow. In the 1930s.

1945年抗战胜利后，国民党当局把蒋介石画像悬挂在南京路、西藏路口的大新公司外墙上。

The giant portrait of Chiang Kai-shek hanging on the wall of The Sun Corporation in 1945.

IN COMMEMORATION
THE NAMING OF YU YA-CHING ROAD.
1st Oct., 1936.

1936年西藏路被命名为虞洽卿路。虞洽卿为上海华人商界领袖，上海租界仅有三条马路以中国人名字命名，虞洽卿路为其中之一。
In 1936, Xizang road was renamed Yuqiaqin Road, the name of a Chinese leader in Shanghai. At that time only three roads were named after Chinese, and Yuqiaqin was one of them.

市井风情
URBAN STYLE

老上海风景　OLD SHANGHAI: A PHOTOGRAPHIC ALBUM

[096] 1920年代的望平街（今山东中路）报馆和出版社云集，这里是上海报纸和书籍的批发、销售集散地。

[096] Publishing Houses gathered on Wangping Road (current Middle Shangdong Road). This place used to be the distributing center of newspaper and books in Shanghai. In the1920s.

[097] 1930年代公共租界南京路上店招遮天蔽日。

[097] The sign-boards on Nanjing Road was so densely hanged that even covered up the sky. In the 1930s.

1890年代虹口。

Hongkou district in the 1890s.

1923年改建的虹口三角地菜场，是当时上海规模最大的室内菜场。
The Sanjiaodi Market in1923. It was the largest indoor market in Shanghai.

徐家汇天主教堂，1910年10月22日举行落成典礼。法国中世纪风格，两侧顶部为哥特式钟楼楼，尖顶，高50米。教堂门窗为尖拱式，镶彩绘玻璃，是中国第一座按西方建筑样式建造的教堂。

The Xujiahui Cathedral, built in 1910 in French mid-age style, the two sides of the cathedral were two gothic bell towers. It is the first Western style church built in China.

徐家汇天主教堂前的中外神职人员合影，摄于1920年代。
Clergymen in front of Xujiahui Cathedral, photo taken in the 1920s.

建成于1907年的上海火车北站。

The Shanghai North Railway Station built in 1907.

建于1930年的霞飞路（今淮海中路）皮恩公寓（图右侧），1956年改为上海妇女用品商店。
The Beam Apartment on Huaihai Road built in 1930. It became the Shanghai women's store in 1956.

1930年代的东长治路街景，中间建筑为日本电信局，现已不存。

The East Changzhi Road in the 1930s. In the middle was the Japanese telecommunication office. This building no longer exists by now.

在上海工作和生活的外国人也会乘坐独轮车上街。摄于1900年代。
Foreigners in Shanghai also took wheelbarrow in the 1900s.

独轮车是上海及周边地区常见的载货载人工具，车上坐着两位富家子弟，前面这位拿着把洋伞，后面的拿着把中国油纸伞，摄于1890年代。

Wheelbarrow was a common transporting vehicle in the area of Shanghai. This photo shows two kids from a rich family sitting on a Wheelbarrow. On their hands were a Chinese oiled paper umbrella and a foreign umbrella. In the 1890s.

1890年代，从东洋引进的黄包车比独轮车乘坐舒适。

Jinrikisha introduced from Japan were more comfortable than wheelbarrow in the 1890s.

1900年代的静安寺。英国人越界筑路，将南京路从跑马厅一直延伸到静安寺，现在的南京西路当时叫静安寺路。

Jing'an Temple in the 1900s. The British at that time overstep the boundary of the settlement and extended Nanjing Road all the way from the Race Club to Jing'an Temple, the current West Nanjing Road in Shanghai was once called Jing'an Si Road.

1908年3月20日，英商有轨电车正式在上海运营，首条线路是从外滩至静安寺。

The streetcar owned by the British went into operation on 20th March, 1908, the first line was from the Bund to Jing'an Temple.

有轨电车站，1930年代。
The streetcar station in 1930s.

RAILLESS CAR (CONTAINING 35 PASSENGERS) OCCUPYING

[112] 1914年英商开通无轨电车线路，以弥补有轨电车运营的不足，但运营情况一直不佳，直到1926年才真正有了第一辆无轨电车。图为行驶在赫德路（今常德路）上的无轨电车。

[112] In order to make up the shortage of streetcar, railless car line was opened up in 1914. But because of the financial situation, the first railless car had not come to Shanghai until 1926. The railless streetcar on Changde Road in the 1920s.

[113] 1934年，英商中国公共汽车公司在上海引进双层公共汽车，轰动一时。

[113] Double-deckers were introduced to Shanghai in 1934.

[114] 17路电车经过西藏路大世界站，1940年代。

[114] The streetcar driving through the Great World Entertainment Center in the 1940s.

[115] 1930年代西藏路跑马厅路段街景。此路原为泥城浜，1914年填浜筑路，初名西藏路，1936年更名虞洽卿路。虞洽卿为上海华人商界领袖，上海租界仅有三条马路以中国人名字命名，虞洽卿路为其中之一。

[115] The street view of the Race Club area of Xizang Road. This road was originally a creek and it was filled in 1914. The road was later renamed Yuqiaqin Road, the name of a Chinese leader in Shanghai. At that time only three roads were named after Chinese, and Yuqiaqin was one of them.Photo was taken in the 1930s.

[116-117] 1940年代福州路上自行车、人力车、三轮车大行其道。

[116-117] Bicycles, rickshaws, and tricycles all in Fuzhou Road in the 1940s.

[118] 1949年，解放前夕的四川北路的车流和人流。

[118] The human and traffic flow on North Sichuan Road the day before the liberation.of Shanghai Photo taken in 1949.

[119] 1948年，国民政府经济接近崩溃，货币贬值严重。图中为替人数钱的银行职员。

[119] In 1948, the economy of the KMT government was collapsing and the currency was seriously devalued. The photo shows a bank clerk counting money.

雨后街头积水。

The East Changzhi Road after a heavy rain in the 1930s.

1930年代大雨后积水的浙江路。
Water was gathered on Zhejiang Road after a heavy rain in the 1930s.

1910年的公共租界南京路外滩码头，旅客在浮桥上候船。
The ferry dock on the Bund, in 1910.

市渡輪每晚八時半由此開行乘涼夜班
MUNICIPAL FERRY SPECIAL NIGHT TRIP. DEP. HERE EVERY NIGHT AT 8.30 P.M.

1930年代的公共租界爱多路外滩浮动码头，当时上海开设了夜班乘凉轮渡，类似于现在的浦江游览。
Floating docks on the Bund, in the 1930s. At that time, a night ferry line was introduced to the Bund, which is similar to the current Huangpu River Curise.

1940年代锦江饭店老楼前草坪上休闲的欧洲侨民。
Foreigners having a leisure time on the front lawn of Jinjiang Hotel in the 1940s.

1940年代公共租界街头电车和行人。

Passengers and a streetcar on the street in the 1940s.

街头织补玻璃丝袜的女子。
The woman repairing socks on the street.

1940年代，小学生在上国语课。
Primary students taking Chinese lessons in the 1940s.

1930年代，法租界马路边遛狗的西侨和拾荒的中国少年。

A dog-walking Westerner and a garbage-collecting Chinese young person on the street of the French Settlement, in the 1930s.

租界马路上三轮车夫为车资与洋人发生争执。

A tricycle wheeler and a Westerner having an argument for the payment on the street.

1940年代上海华界街头的交通警察和行人。
The passengers and traffic policeman on the street in the 1940s.

1940年代上海街头的修车摊和正在休息的三轮车夫。
Rickshaw pullers resting on the street in the 1940s.

［132］ 1940年代街头月份牌画售卖。

[132] Calendar poster on the street in the1940.

［133］ 1940年代街头连环画摊点。

[133] Street stalls for Chinese comic books in the 1940s.

1940年代，支架在当铺边的和连环画摊点。

Pawnshops and street stalls for Chinese comic books in the 1940s.

1940年代大光明电影院外墙的巨幅海报。

Huge posters outside the Grand Theatre, in the 1940s.

[136] 1948年，绘有好莱坞明星的街头广告。
[136] Street commercials and movie posters on the street in1948.
[137] 1948年，街头广告和电影海报。
[137] Street commercials and movie posters on the street in1948.

[138] 1930年代，穿旗袍的三姐妹。

[138] Modern girls with Cheongsam dress in the 1930s.

[139] 1926年，上海百乐门舞厅内翩翩起舞的男女舞客。

[139] People dancing with the rhythm inside Paramount Dance Hall in 1926.

1920年代，国民政府提倡新文化运动，女性得到了更多的受教育机会，图为上海充满自信和喜悦的知识女性。

The Guomingdang Government advocated the New Cultural Movement in the 1920s. Women got more opportunities in receiving education, this photo shows the women of the new generation, with happiness and confidence.

1948年，悠闲的华界街头报纸、杂志摊贩。

Newspaper and magazine agent on the street in 1948.

上海解放前夕，国民党当局一面负隅顽抗，一面制造虚假繁荣，图为大世界门口密集的广告。

Before the liberation of Shanghai, the KMT government was busy fighting and making false prosperity. The photo shows the massive advertising board at the entrance of the Great World in 1949.

1949年10月2日，庆祝上海解放，人民解放军在老公共租界工部局楼顶升起中华人民共和国五星红旗。

On October 2nd, 1949, the Five-starred Red Flag rising at the top of the old Public Settlement Municipal Council after the liberation of Shanghai.

图书在版编目（CIP）数据

老上海风景 / 汤伟康编著. —上海：上海人民美术出版社，2018.2
ISBN 978-7-5586-0702-8

Ⅰ.①老… Ⅱ.①汤… Ⅲ. ①上海市－地方史－史料－图集
Ⅳ.①K295.1-64

中国版本图书馆CIP数据核字（2018）第034102号

老上海风景

撰　　文：汤伟康
翻　　译：刘　权
责任编辑：刘晓天
技术编辑：季　卫
装帧设计：杨宗雄
出版发行：上海人民美术出版社
　　　　　（上海长乐路672弄33号）
印　　刷：上海丽佳制版印刷有限公司
开　　本：889×1194　1/24　6印张
版　　次：2018年3月第1版
印　　次：2018年3月第1次
印　　数：0001-2000
书　　号：ISBN 978-7-5586-0702-8
定　　价：88.00元

我们已经尽力寻找本书图片的作者，但仍有部分作者未能落实，特此深表歉意。
请有关作者或版权所有者见书后与我们联系，以便奉寄稿酬。